Creating Homeschool Balance

Find Harmony Between
Type A and Type Zzz ...

Lee Binz,
The HomeScholar

First Printing, 2015

Printed in the United States of America

ISBN: 1511435518
ISBN-13: 978-1511435512

Disclaimer: Parents assume full responsibility for the education of their children in accordance with state law. College requirements vary, so make sure to check with the colleges about specific requirements for homeschoolers. We offer no guarantees, written or implied, that the use of our products and services will result in college admissions or scholarship awards.

Creating Homeschool Balance

Find Harmony Between
Type A and Type Zzz ...

What are Coffee Break Books?

Creating Homeschool Balance is part of The HomeScholar's Coffee Break Book series.

Designed especially for parents who don't want to spend hours and hours reading a 400-page book on homeschooling high school, each book combines Lee's practical and friendly approach with detailed, but easy-to-digest information, perfect to read over a cup of coffee at your favorite coffee shop!

Never overwhelming, always accessible and manageable, each book in the series will give parents the tools they need to tackle the tasks of homeschooling high school, one warm sip at a time.

Everything about these Coffee Break Books is designed to connote simplicity, ease, and comfort - from the size (fits in a purse), to the font and paragraph length (easy on the eyes), to the price (the same as a Starbucks Venti Triple Caramel Macchiato). Unlike a fancy coffee drink, however, these books are guilt-free pleasures you will want to enjoy again and again!

Table of Contents

Introduction

Goldilocks Homeschooling

How do you know if you're doing too much, too little, or just the right amount of schoolwork in your homeschool? Sometimes it's hard to tell. Because "too much" and "too little" mean different things to different people, depending on their circumstances, a better goal to strive for is balance.

Try to find the sweet spot between doing too much and too little. Sometimes balance can be elusive. It might help to think about the story of "Goldilocks and the Three Bears." Your "just right" is not something another person can choose for you, because just as everyone has their own preferred porridge temperature, we each have our own individual circumstances and goals. Your homeschool balance will be unique to you.

Another good analogy involves a Starbucks latte; everybody has a favorite Starbucks coffee, and everybody has their own specific preferences. Tall, Grande, Venti, with whip or without, regular or low fat — the possibilities are endless and unique to each person. Your homeschool balance is like that, too.

Even though it's unique, it's important. I hope that within the pages of this book, you will find some ideas to help you and your family find a balance that is just right for you.

Chapter 1

Strategies to Create Balance

What does "too much" look like? Doing too much makes homeschoolers feel completely overwhelmed. It's when you, your husband, and your children are tired all the time; you're terribly behind, can't possibly catch up, and the curriculum is incredibly intense.

On the other hand, some parents do too little. They don't seem to get to reading, writing, or math, all the children want to do is play video games, and nothing educational seems to happen in their homeschool. You might be doing too little if you engage in less than four hours of educational activity (not just bookwork) a day.

Morning Meeting

Oops. They were supposed to be working independently. Instead, they goofed off.

Never under-estimate a teenager's ability to avoid work. While sometimes they have intentional lapses, many times teens are focused on other priorities (such as hair or new shoes) and they forget trivial things such as math assignments or research reports.

It would be nice to have teenagers grow up one day and suddenly BE responsible, but it's unlikely. It's more common for teenagers to BECOME responsible over time. It takes a lot of time and practice, often with constant time spent shaping and molding. Kids don't start the first day of ninth grade as responsible adults; they BEGIN the process of becoming responsible adults.

That's where the morning meeting can help. When you start the morning by checking in with your child each day, you can shape and mold their "responsibility index." A quick 15 or 30-minute check in with each child can give you the time needed to assess the situation and correct the behavior, encouraging your child to take more responsibility as you go.

Go over what you expect of your child, or discuss the schoolwork they did yesterday. Just touch base briefly on each of their subjects. It's not instruction time, because you don't have to teach your children everything when you homeschool. Your goal is for them to be able to learn independently. It's a time to touch base and make sure they're on task, not overwhelmed, and doing the work they're supposed to do. It's also a time for you to be accountable; know what subjects they need to cover and follow up with your children.

The morning meeting can help your child stay on task, so they don't "forget" school for a week (or a month!) and fall hopelessly behind. A daily meeting is a great goal. In practice, though, you will miss a day here and there. We are all busy people with busy lives, after all! But if you forget a day or two, you will still benefit. Any meeting can provide feedback for children. If you miss a few days, you will eventually return to a meeting and discover any missed assignments.

Even in the "real world" after school, adults encounter frequent check-ups. In business, employees often have a daily meeting with employers. A meeting may not ALWAYS happen, but if it USUALLY happens, it can help catch any missed assignments.

Weak Areas

Another key to finding balance in your homeschool is to put your weak areas first. Figure out your children's academically weak areas, and work on those courses first each day. If your child's weak area is math, prioritize math. If you recognize your own weak area is organization, that's how you need to prioritize your time.

Put your weak area first in terms of your time, so the subject your child isn't good at becomes the first thing done during the day. It's your number one priority, and you don't do anything just for fun until you've taken care of the weak area.

Also put your weak area first in terms of your money. Your weak area should be the first thing you spend money on when you go to a convention and buy curriculum. Allow yourself to re-purchase curriculum in your weak area if the curriculum you chose isn't working.

If yours or your child's weak area is math, put math first. Ensure it is completed before anything else. It comes first; it's the number one subject and you won't let it go. Even if somebody gives you free tickets to the theater, don't go unless you get math done first. It's the first thing you do with your money and your time.

Chapter 2

Doing Too Much

In order to determine whether you're doing too much, evaluate yourself first, because "too much" can look different depending on what your homeschool is like. For most people, too much is doing too many hours of school. Too much also means you recognize stress and anxiety in yourself, and you feel like hitting your head against the wall. Sometimes a friend or a teacher will warn you. One of my clients told me that all of her friends felt she was doing too much, and she needed help slowing down. She heard these warnings, but she hadn't been taking them seriously.

You also know you're doing too much when your spouse is concerned.

Sometimes they feel things aren't working out as well as expected. If your spouse says you're doing too much in your homeschool, you probably are.

Another way you'll know is when your children complain. Of course, children will complain in general, but if they're complaining a lot about having too much schoolwork, and how they can't possibly get it all done, listen to them. It may be the case. You may have chosen a curriculum that is a mismatch; it is either above grade level or below grade level, and not something you can reasonably expect of your children.

When there are not enough hours in the day to complete your homeschool work, and everybody tells you it's too much, you need to listen – it's not something to laugh off. Overload can beat the love of learning out of your children. If people try to communicate this message, pay attention.

Hurrying High School

One of the causes of doing too much is trying to fit four years of high school into a single year. Some parents think their child has to know how to write a research report, an essay, poetry, use college level vocabulary, and complete all of their spelling by October of freshman year. That's not going to happen! You can't fit four years of high school into one year.

Remember when your child was a newborn, and then think about them as a four-year-old. There is a big difference between a newborn and a four-year-old. A four-year-old can do many things a newborn can't do — they can play independently for a short period of time and not only walk, but run. The difference between a freshman and a senior is similar. You can't expect them to do the same amount of work, so be careful when a curriculum claims it is designed for a junior or senior. Don't use it with a freshman unless you're confident they're ready.

Don't try to cram all of high school into one year. Spread it out evenly. That's probably the biggest solution to hurrying high school — work on just one year of school each year. Set some time limits for yourself. If you tend to be a person that does too much, watch the clock to see whether you are spending too long on each subject.

Math and English

There are two subjects that tend to take a particularly long time to complete: math and English. Be realistic. Math problems can take a while, because most homeschoolers use a video tutorial (since most homeschool moms don't know how to do calculus). Watching math videos and working on assignments takes time.

English is similar. It's important to cover both reading and writing every day, and each takes time. Whether your child is a reluctant reader who takes a while to read a short passage, or a prolific reader who you just can't pull a book away from, reading and writing is going to take a bit of time.

Time Limits

Make sure to limit other subjects to one hour each. For instance, work on social studies for an hour, foreign language for an hour — whatever you do, just no more than an hour each. No matter what you pack into high school history, keep it to one hour and don't go overtime. Watching the clock can help you avoid overworking your children. Sometimes the tendency with history is to consider it fun, and then spend three or four hours on it, which means you don't have time to get math done. By setting time limits for each subject, you can work through them a bit faster.

For a reality check, consider what would be required on the job for an adult. Usually, adults work 8-hour days. If your child works more than the hours expected of a full-time job, that's too much by any measure. Don't homeschool more than eight hours each day, because that is the equivalent of a full-time job for you, too.

Delight Directed Learning

Delight directed learning is slightly different from ordinary schoolwork. If your child wants to keep reading at night, or wants to keep doing P.E. at night, then that's fine. You can exceed the eight hours per day if it includes delight directed learning.

Keep in mind that for delight directed learning, you don't direct the class. Delight directed learning means the child directs the class and decides what's fun for them. This type of class isn't about mom deciding what's fun for mom; it's about the child's interests. You also don't have to make delight directed learning into a high school subject. Your children can just learn on their own.

If they love the piano, you don't have to sit down and create a fill-in-the-bubble test, or create midterms and finals for piano class. You can just let them learn to play the piano. At the end, you can collect all of those activities, include them in a course description, and give your child high school credit. If your child loves economics, collect all the books they've read and include them as primary texts in your course description. If they're writing economics papers for fun, include all of the papers they wrote in your course description. Let them determine how long they work on delight directed learning each day!

Chapter 3

Tyranny of the Urgent

One enemy of homeschool balance is the tyranny of the urgent. You may start to feel as if there are too many urgent tasks, and torn between multiple commitments. This can easily happen when you sign up for too many activities. Homeschoolers have many wonderful opportunities to choose from, because we have the freedom to choose great activities during the day in addition to evening activities. Activities can be wonderful, but the truth is you can't do them all, because you will end up being spread too thin.

Some homeschoolers who succumb to this imbalance are "do-gooders" – people who try to do good works for the world. It's wonderful to do good works, volunteer work, such as serving at church. But, you have to be careful to prioritize. Do-gooders feel guilty if they're not volunteering multiple hours by fundraising, delivering for Meals on Wheels, involved in church leadership, or if their child isn't engaged in excessive hours of community service. Remember your focus and purpose is educating and raising your children. Sometimes the tyranny of the urgent can seem most important, but it's not your primary mission.

Think about what you're truly trying to accomplish; figure out what your real priorities are. They probably include serving the community, but that's not your number one priority. Homeschooling is your vocation – it's the job you have chosen. You've put other things aside to commit to this vocation, so you need to focus.

Look at your activities as filling a time bucket. Place the big rocks in the bucket first. If you put your real priorities in your time bucket first, there is still space to include other things that are not your first priority, but are still urgent. On the other hand, if you fill your time bucket up with the urgent things first, there may not be any room for what's truly important – your commitment to homeschooling.

Keep a to-do list and when your priority (homeschooling) is done for the day or your students can work independently for an hour, go through the list of tasks that seem urgent at the time. You have to prioritize instead of just doing what comes up during the day. Otherwise, by the end of the week, you won't have done any homeschooling.

Chapter 4

Below Grade Level

Some people find themselves doing too much in their homeschool when their child is behind their grade level. Parents may try so hard to compensate for weaknesses (usually the child's weaknesses), that they overwork their child in that particular area. If your child struggles with reading, the temptation is to force them to learn to read for three hours a day. As you can imagine, this can cause burnout. Burnout leads to children who no longer love learning. Thus, it's important to avoid overcompensating for weaknesses by doing too much, or spending excessive amounts of time on weak subjects.

If you have a child who is behind grade level in a subject, overcompensating can lead to self-esteem issues. If a child starts to recognize Mom's anxiety and feels terrible about what they can do, or says, "I feel stupid" or "I can't learn," you may be overworking them. If your child is below grade level, work on any areas that need improvement, but not every day, and not every subject every day. Keep each subject to a reasonable amount of time.

Learning Difficulties

It's a good idea to separate your child's learning process from their weaknesses whenever possible. For instance, if your child has trouble physically writing — perhaps they have dysgraphia — don't require them to write for other subjects. Just have them narrate answers to you, provide them with an oral test, or have them work on the computer instead of using a pencil. Separate their weaknesses from as many other subject areas as possible.

Dyslexia is another learning challenge that can cause problems. If your student has trouble with reading, work on reading comprehension for a reasonable amount of time during English class. Make sure you don't require reading for more than half an hour to an hour a day, so your student doesn't become overly frustrated. At the same time, separate dyslexia from other subjects; don't make your child work on reading for an hour every day AND require reading for history or chemistry. For subjects that involve reading and writing, use videos, read aloud to your student, or substitute projects for writing instead. When a child has dyslexia, a public or private school often provides an assistant who reads aloud to them, and that's just one of the ways you can help your child compensate.

.

Chapter 4

Grandiose Thinking

Another cause of overwork and homeschool imbalance is what I call grandiose thinking, or over-ambitious goals. Remember, no one can do it all (not and stay healthy)! The solution to thinking you can do it all is to moderate yourself and set realistic goals. If you are covering the core classes of English, social studies, science, foreign language, math, and fine arts, you are doing enough. You don't need more than one credit in each subject each year.

In addition to core courses, try to capture your student's delight whenever possible. Remember though, it's their delight. If they love music, don't try to teach them piano, orchestra, and music history all at the same time, thinking they'll love it. Capture their delight, but don't overwork them with unrealistic goals.

If you feel overworked, look at the number of subjects you're teaching to see whether you're trying to cover seven or more subjects in a day. That would be an overly ambitious goal! One solution is to alternate subjects that are semester-long courses. Some courses, such as economics or American government, are often one-semester or half-year classes. Other subjects only need to be taught for one year, such as fine art, or two to three years, such as foreign language. Alternate short-term classes so you don't try to cover them all at once.

Too Much

Using too much curriculum will also lead to overwork and lack of balance. Book hoarders or curriculum junkies have bookshelves filled with curriculum for all the grade levels they've completed, will do, or will have grandchildren do in the future! One of the problems of owning every curriculum under the sun is that homeschoolers want to use it all. They tend to mix-and-match. When you hodge-podge your curriculum together, it can cause overwork. If you have 58 different readings on the first year of the American Revolution, you'll never get past the first year of the American Revolution!

Of course, your intentions are good; you're searching for that perfect curriculum, recognizing that each child is unique. The problem is that you end up trying to use all the curriculum, which is crazy. The solution is not to use it all. Although it's important to invest in your weaknesses, you don't have to invest in everything. You don't need six different kinds of curriculum to teach Algebra 1.

Supplementing the Supplements

Another source of overwork is supplementing your supplements. Homeschoolers do this all the time. If you end up supplementing a curriculum that is already too big, it quickly becomes huge. This is especially true if you are using a full curriculum such as *Sonlight* or *Tapestry of Grace*. To avoid overwork, every time you supplement remember to take something out. If one thing goes in, then something else comes out every single time, no matter what it is. If you have free tickets to the theater to see "1776," that's great, but you can't add it to your curriculum unless you subtract something.

All for One

When it comes to curriculum, it's important to remember that just because you bought something for your child doesn't mean you have to use it. I know this goes against our innate thriftiness as homeschoolers, but you're just setting yourself up for failure if you don't heed this advice. The same is true if you bought something for one child, and think you must use it for all your other children. The curriculum may be a good fit for your visual learner, but may be an utter failure for the next child, who is an auditory learner. If you love a particular curriculum but it's not a good fit for your child, don't use it!

Double Trouble

Another way to avoid burnout is to make sure you don't double up in subject areas. Many homeschoolers would like to have their child learn math with perfect mastery, and assign twice as many math problems as required each day, using two different books. The child typically doesn't finish math by the end of the year because they've doubled up and done twice as much. This is too much! The only exception is if the subject area is your child's delight directed learning. Remember, even though you have a child that loves music, one music course per year could be the right amount, even if it's purely through delight directed learning. In general, don't double up your curriculum, especially if it's your idea. The only time I recommend doubling up is when the idea comes from the child and is something they want to do.

Chapter 6

Perfectionism

Many homeschool parents struggle with perfectionism; it's a leading cause of doing too much. We want so much to be a good educator that we try to make our homeschool look too much like "school," and teach everything the hard way. If your homeschool looks much like school-at-home, including many textbooks, and words like "syllabus" and "rubric" are a regular part of your vocabulary, watch out for the pitfalls of perfectionism.

Education does not require perfectionism. You don't have to finish every single problem in every book. In science class, for example, perfectionism looks like stopping ten times per paragraph and asking your child the definition of all the words. The next thing you know, you've demanded two hours of blood, sweat, and tears per class. It's okay to seek mastery in homeschooling, but that's not the same as perfectionism. I personally have mastery over addition, subtraction, multiplication, and division, but that does not mean I'm perfect. I've messed up my checkbook many times, since I'm not as careful at those tasks as I used to be. Mastery is not the same as perfection. Learning may not require that your child complete every single problem in the chapter — they may do just as well by finishing just the odd or even problems.

The solution to this problem is to be ruthless and start cutting things out. Teachers in schools learn how to cut parts of a curriculum they don't want to or don't have time to cover; they decide in advance which 20% of the curriculum they're not going to cover. You can do that, too. Homeschoolers usually start the year assuming they will finish the whole curriculum, but there may come a time when they wonder whether they're ever going to be done with science or history. Look at your curriculum, and decide that the 20% at the end of your book is the 20% you're not going to finish.

Popcorn Party

The "End of Year Popcorn Party Plan" is another strategy I like to use to combat perfectionism. If you recognize there's no way to finish school and maintain your sanity, you want to finish up quickly but you're a perfectionist, break out the popcorn. Quickly finish your subjects using videos and audios. For example, if you are studying American history, you could watch Ken Burns' documentary about the Civil War for your Civil War studies. You could quickly cover the Oregon Trail by watching a movie about it as well. The next thing you know, you're good to go.

Hard and Easy Classes

Some classes are easier than others are. Math and English each often take more than an hour to cover — not all the time, but sometimes. Not all of your classes need to be difficult. When I was in high school, we called the easy classes "Underwater Basket Weaving." It's okay for some homeschool classes to be easier than others are as well. While in general it's not helpful to base your academic guidelines on the public school standard, remember that not all of your homeschool classes need to be academically rigorous.

One of my friends teaches cheerleading after school, and her young cheerleader friends told her about the high school occupational education credit they were earning. All they had to do was bake frozen cookie dough. Someone else was in charge of taking the cookies and packaging them, selling them at the school, and managing the money and the banking. For baking frozen cookie dough, they each received one credit of occupational education. That would be an example of an "Underwater Basket Weaving" class! While most homeschoolers wouldn't use this as a standard for any class, it does show that not all classes need to be as difficult as English or math.

One of my clients went to her local public school and watched a P.E. class for 50 days. All the children in that class did was sit on the sideline and wait for the teacher. He talked to them for a while, but most of the time he did nothing — they did not break a sweat, and they were only out there for 30 minutes. That was their P.E. class. Sometimes homeschoolers think we should force our children to run a mile every day! It's okay not to be over the top in every class.

If you are a perfectionist, your job is to say "No" to some great things. There is simply too much wonderful stuff to do, and it is not possible for you to say "Yes" to everything. You have to be ruthless and cut anything that's too much. You have to pick and choose. That's hard for a perfectionist, but it's the only way to maintain your sanity.

Chapter 7

Doing Too Little

Two kinds of people tend to say they do too little. One is the person who works all day long and accomplishes a lot of homeschool work every day, but feels they do too little. The second kind of person is the one who actually does too little work.

Too Little Focus

If you think you do too little, consider what you do each day, and whether you describe yourself as busy all day long. Would you say that you engage in educational activities, but don't do homeschool work? Many times, this indicates a lack of focus. Homeschoolers can get distracted by the small stuff.

They start baking a cake and the next thing you know, they're cake decorating, and schoolwork takes a backseat. Homeschoolers also get distracted by small things such as leadership, finances, or faith development. These are very important, but if they're the only things done each day, then you're not getting schoolwork done. The small things can add up. It's not that you're doing too little; the problem is prioritizing and trying to get things in the right order.

The solution to this problem is to solve your misperceptions first. Then recognize that you are working all day long on educational activities. You simply need to re-adjust your priorities. Think about what is important, and put those subjects first. Core classes are important in your homeschool: reading, writing, math, science, and social studies. Once you've put those subjects in, put in all the "urgent" things, such as finances, leadership, and faith development.

Too Little School

Some parents simply don't require enough schoolwork. How do you know when it's truly a problem? You hear your kids (or spouse) say, "We aren't really doing reading, writing, or math." That's a good tip that you're not doing enough schoolwork. Playing video games all day can sometimes be a cause.

Another much more serious cause of too little schoolwork can be any tremendous family crisis, such as a major hospitalization, divorce, or sudden deployment. These family crises may leave you feeling overwhelmed or paralyzed.

If you've had a family crisis, you may have kept up with school, but sometimes, when life is horrendous, that's not possible. At that point, you should probably forgive yourself and accept where you are. To solve the problem of doing too little, re-evaluate where you are. If you recognize that you aren't doing much schoolwork, decide to re-evaluate and make a reasonable plan going forward. Can your children read and do math? What level have they achieved in math? Are they at grade level in reading? Have they learned because they love reading, even when not doing schoolwork? An assessment will help you make a reasonable plan going forward.

One of my clients did too little school as a result of a multitude of factors — too many video games, not using any curriculum, and a family crisis. Even while she was in the midst of the crisis and gave no direction on schoolwork, her children were learning incessantly about American history, because that's what they read for fun. When she began assessing where they were, it was easy to see that they got their American history covered. Other people might never do it that way, but they still did it!

Try to find that balance between doing too much and doing too little, especially during times of stress, or when making a huge change. If the family hasn't been doing schoolwork and you need to get started, make small steps to begin moving forward.

Chapter 8

Finding Balance

One of the best ways to incorporate balance in your homeschool is to make room for margin. When you open up a book, the wide blank margin around the edges makes it easier to read. If the words went right up to the edges of the paper, it would be difficult to read. In the same way, life is easier to live when you leave room for margin. If you fill your day from beginning to end with activity, it will be more difficult to maintain your personal sanity while you homeschool. This is especially true if you've come out of a family crisis, or you've never homeschooled before. If you overdo it, it's going to come back to bite you.

If you're just barely back on your feet after a crisis, or you are just starting to homeschool, try to keep your hours reasonable. Homeschooling for up to six hours is the absolute most you want to spend. At the same time, if you've done too little schoolwork, and try to compensate by doing 12 hours of homeschool every day, that will cause nothing but problems.

Like a book, life works best when you have a nice, wide margin around each day. Although you may be working hard, you're not working from sun-up until sundown. Of course, you don't want entirely blank pages. Don't leave your child without an education.

Leaving room for margin is an important life skill to teach your children. Your good example demonstrates that they don't have to work from six in the morning until ten at night. Working during the day is an important work ethic skill to develop. While it's okay to have children work every day, you don't want them to work themselves to the bone. You want them to complete their tasks, but not become completely overwhelmed.

Core and Delight

The solution to doing too little is similar to the solution to doing too much. Cover the core classes every single day: reading, writing, math, history, and science. Then capture delight, the subjects that your children just learn naturally, without any effort on your part. There are kids who play electric guitar for hours on end; that's delight directed learning of music, and you don't have to teach them piano at the same time. Some children's delight directed learning might include riding their bike, which you can count as P.E.

A second solution to doing too little is to hold a morning meeting. Touch base with each of your children each day to make sure they're on task. You might miss your morning meeting once or twice a week, but if you try to get it in every day, they can't forget their math for two months at a time. This will help your child stay focused on what they need to do. Your first priorities are reading, writing, and math. Your second priorities are social studies, science, and foreign language. Make sure you get core classes done, and then capture delight directed courses by recording activities they like doing on their own.

Calculating Credit

It could be a misperception that you're doing too little. I encourage you to start counting credits by books. If you finish a textbook, give your student one credit. If you feel like you did too little, but your student completed Algebra 1, and they are ready for Algebra 2, you can count the books they finished and give them one credit each.

You can also count credits by the hour. If you feel like you're doing too little because you're not directing your children, look at what they work on for hours. If your student has completed 120 to 180 hours of work, count it as a one-credit class. Don't worry, you don't have to painstakingly record every hour. If your child works for an hour a day on a subject, that typically adds up to a one-credit class.

If you bought a history curriculum, used it, and supplemented like crazy, don't give your student a failing grade because you didn't get to the second half of the curriculum. Give them a grade based on what they did. They worked hard for the whole school year, and didn't finish the curriculum because you piled too much on, but they worked for about 180 hours. If they understood it, you can give them a grade of A. Don't give them a lower grade just because they didn't finish a curriculum.

Choose Carefully and Face Fears

Choose your curriculum carefully. Think about your child's learning style as well as your teaching style, and try to find a curriculum that's not a mismatch. Sometimes a curriculum mismatch is the cause of doing too little. If a student hates their math book, for example, they will avoid math. Find a book that matches their learning style and your teaching style instead, and it will probably help.

Another solution to doing too little is to face your fears. Sometimes people do too little because they're afraid if they finish science this year, they'll be that much closer to having to do a scary physics class next year. Face your fears, and be fearless about upper level subjects! The first time I took the Calculus class in college, my grade point was 0.7. Thankfully, I met my husband, and he helped me study calculus. The second time I took the Calculus class, I earned 3.7! I still didn't understand what any of the symbols meant, but I did earn a good enough grade to move forward!

I was terrified of teaching calculus in my homeschool. We bought a curriculum that came with a video tutorial so that I didn't have to teach anything. My kids watched the video tutorial, worked on the problems in the book, looked at the answer key when they were ready to check each answer, and then reworked the problems if needed. Then I took away the answer key and gave them a test. I didn't know what the symbols meant in the answer key, but I compared their test and the answer key side-by-side. If their answers did not look anything like the answer key, I just marked them wrong. If my children fussed (since they were perfectionists), I told them to call the 800-number to find out if their answer was correct. I wouldn't mark it correct unless I heard otherwise from that 800-number, which put the ball in their court!

When I read books to my children in our homeschool, I felt like I needed to understand the content, but you don't need to. If your child has dyslexia, and you read their lessons aloud, you don't have to understand everything. They have to understand, and work on the problems. You can even let them answer problems orally if needed.

Let your children learn on their own. Give them the test, take away the answer key, check their test, and make sure the answers are just right. I was terrified of upper level subjects, but I managed to ensure my children learned calculus and physics. They learned Latin too, even though I still don't know Latin. Don't let fear hold your children (or you!) back; face your fear instead.

Not Perfection

At the same time, don't expect perfect understanding. You're not going to find perfection in your children, or in yourself. Don't be afraid if they don't attain 100% mastery. They may never get to 100% and may only get to 80 or 90%. Keep moving forward. High school is not about college-level learning, you just want your student to work at a high school level.

Expect your child to need practice. They're not always going to get it right. Think about football practice. The coach will have them run the plays, but they won't always get them right. The practice, however, helps them be ready for game day. The amount of practice will vary, since some kids will need more than others do.

Forward Momentum

Your goal in homeschooling is to continue with your forward momentum — keep moving through subjects. Don't over-compensate for weaknesses. If your child is weak in English, don't beat them up by piling on grammar, punctuation, and diagramming sentences. That tends to squash your child's love of learning. Some students understand more fully when subjects are less complicated, and presented simply and slowly. Piling on the work destroys momentum.

Gaps

Avoiding gaps is another strategy for finding balance. Some students are drawn into art and English, and are talented at anything artistic or word-oriented. For them, these subjects are easy. These students sometimes have gaps in math and science. For them, make sure you cover math and science every single day. Chances are they're going to engage in artistic pursuits over the summer or during the evenings, and will easily cover an art credit. It's more difficult to convince them to do math and science! Working on these subjects every day can help. Just like it's important to put weak areas first, if you identify that math and science are hard for your child, work on them daily, and don't leave gaps.

Chapter 9

Seasonal Stressors

Another problem you might run into when doing too much or too little is the stress of the seasons. The winter holidays — Thanksgiving until New Year's Day — can be difficult. There's also the time period around January and February when people become sick to death of school! January and February are when teachers in public schools burn out, so it's only natural that you may feel burned out, too. You may also feel seasonal panic to finish the year, which usually happens between March and May. The worst stressor happens during senior year, when families panic over finishing the last year of high school, in June. That particular seasonal stressor can be quite difficult.

Spring Fever

Sometimes homeschoolers feel freaked out and break down, or have a panic attack because they feel like they're falling behind. They think there's no way they'll ever be able to catch up, and that they're beyond hope. It's this kind of generalized anxiety on the part of both parents and children that can make them feel anxious about either doing too much or too little.

One way to make sure you hear and understand your children's or your spouse's feelings is to utilize the acronym HUA – heard, understood, acknowledged. Sometimes just reflecting back to them that you have heard them, and that you understand and acknowledge their burn out can help.

Pacing yourself is also important. If you pack in 12-14 hours of school each day because you're trying to finish up, you will cause even more burn out, and become even more frustrated and anxious. Instead, pace yourself, be consistent, and try not to be in a big hurry.

If it's not too late in the year, you may still have time to organize the rest of your year. Decide which subjects you aren't going to pursue and which areas to focus on instead. If you need help organizing the rest of your year, I recommend the book *Managers of Their Homes* by Teri Maxwell. It helped me to reorganize my homeschool many times.

What "Done" Means

If you're dealing with spring fever, you may want to rethink what "done" means. "Done" can mean you've finished 80% of the curriculum. If this is the year your child only completes 80% of the curriculum, even though you've always ensured they finished it in the past, then that's okay. If your teens are causing tremendous frustration and it's just not worth the fight anymore, just call the curriculum done if you've finished 80%. Does it affect your mental health? Weigh the pros and cons of finishing. Sometimes subjects urgently need attention, but sometimes it's not required high school credit, and the cost is enormous stress. Weigh the pros and cons!

This is especially important if you have a senior. Remember, if your senior was in public or private school, they would be done with high school in June. They wouldn't continue to do schoolwork until August, they would just graduate. In the same way, you can let your senior finish if they've completed 80%. Try not to panic, and instead rethink what "done" means.

Summer School

Summer school is another solution to seasonal stresses. Some families homeschool year round, so they don't have the stress of having to finish everything between September and June. Summer school might involve sports, summer camps, or activities that you can put on a transcript. For instance, if your child takes art classes in the summer, they probably don't need to do an art course during the school year.

If your child is involved in many sports during the summer, you probably don't need to schedule P.E. as a class during the school year; just give them credit for what they've accomplished during the summer.

Summer school can also help you complete shorter courses or parts of a course in a painless way. If you're doing too much during the school year, but you feel it's important your children have a short course, such as health or personal finance, as part of their education, you can cover it during the summer.

To avoid burnout, I suggest you set a time limit, because some people will do too much over the summer, too! Limit yourself to just two hours of school each day, to make sure you don't burn your kids out. They need a break too, just as we parents do.

If a subject does need to be done this summer, try to let your children work independently. Independently means you don't teach them, they can learn on their own. If they need some accountability, have them show you their work from across the room, if necessary.

If you do too little schoolwork during the school year, summer can be a good time to catch up on a few core classes. Your child could work on math, or maybe they need to prioritize reading or writing. Spending a few hours each day during the summer could help your student catch up on a few core courses, and help lessen the stress of being behind.

One homeschool mother told me her son had avoided math most of the school year and was hopelessly behind – that's a good reason to continue math during the summer. Only do one lesson per day though, not two! Choose peace!

Another mother was stressed about starting Latin during the summer. It's not worth the stress! Unless you desperately need foreign language credits, choose peace! Skip the foreign language during the summer.

A homeschool dad wondered about reading. Summer is a great time to snuggle up with a book, but don't worry about literary analysis. Grab books from my "College Bound Reading List" on The HomeScholar website. Save those library receipts! That's how you'll collect all the information for your child's reading list as part of your homeschool records. Choose peace, and just enjoy reading this summer.

Parents often ask about working on SAT preparation over the summer. I loved working on a little SAT prep each day, to keep the skills fresh. It doesn't require parental supervision – it's just working through a high school level workbook! Do some SAT prep during the summer, but keep it small, just one section per day, so kids don't rebel. Choose peace – one section per day only takes about half an hour!

Christmas School

Each year, during the month of December, we covered academics lightly in our homeschool. I called it "Christmas School." I covered the core classes first. We worked on reading, writing, and math that built on each other. I also found that Christmas school was a good time to continue studying weak areas, to ensure the skills weren't lost.

To lighten up your holiday workload, try to eliminate some of your "fluff" courses. Remember, it's important to preserve your sanity and prioritize your own mental health. You can't do everything you normally do in addition to extra Christmas activities. It's okay to take a temporary break from some of the usual schoolwork during this period. You can get back to it in January!

Our Christmas School usually involved fun activities, such as crafts and making gifts. You can count these activities for art credit, even in high school. Holiday baking can become part of a culinary art class, for instance. Of course, Christmas School activities such as wrapping or Christmas shopping cannot be put on a transcript. Other skills are valuable, worthwhile life skills, whether included on the transcript or not, such as instruction in financial literacy as you talk about a gift budget.

Finding Balance

What does finding balance look like? It looks different for each family, but it generally feels like peace. You may feel challenged within the perfect balance, but balance will not lead to feeling completely overwhelmed. Balance means you feel busy, but not frantic. It means your kids are learning, but aren't tied to books all day, and your homeschool doesn't look like school at home.

Balance means you're able to engage in activities outside your homeschool, but you're not so busy shuttling the kids around in the car that you can't catch your breath. It means you have a reasonably tidy home, but not in an obsessive-compulsive way. You also have a generally well-fed family because you do cook from time to time. You may not be a gourmet cook, but you do have time to cook meals and eat them together.

Lastly, finding balance means you also have time for yourself. Even if everyone else is doing well, if you are not, things usually fall apart. The old saying, "If Mama ain't happy, ain't nobody happy" is never truer than in your homeschool! Care for yourself as well as your family, and include your own needs in the quest for homeschool balance!

Conclusion

7 Point Sanity-Saving Checklist

Still overwhelmed? I thought I would conclude with a brief Sanity-Saving Checklist to refer to if you feel you're getting out of balance during the school year. This tool will help you keep a lid on your expectations and stress level.

1. Are there enough hours in the day?

It's possible you have purchased 18 hours' worth of curriculum, but I don't suggest you homeschool for 18 hours a day.

2. Will it cause burnout?

If your curriculum is above your child's ability level, or you are using too much curriculum for their needs, then it can cause serious burnout. Don't give too much work in your child's weak area, or they will become frustrated and spiral into negative self-talk.

3. Are kids responsible?

Whenever possible, encourage your children to learn independently. Just remember that independence doesn't happen overnight; the process takes years of training, modeling, and encouragement.

4. Are you expecting too much?

If you are planning to homeschool longer than the average adult's workday, that's too much! Scale back, and limit yourself to a reasonable amount for each subject, starting with core classes first.

5. Did you over-estimate mornings?

Oh sure, we'd all like to say we get up at 6:00 am to start our day, but if your homeschool plans are dependent on making a night owl into a morning person, it just won't work. Don't over estimate what time you (or your child) become functional each morning.

6. Can they concentrate that long?

The reason schools are organized into 50-minute classes is that studies show it's as long as a teenager can concentrate. Mix things up a bit, and don't ask your kids to work on one subject for more than an hour at a time.

7. Could you do it as an adult?

Think about this! If I told you to sit still, without fidgeting, and pay attention to a computer screen or textbook for eight hours straight, could you do it? I don't think so! If you couldn't or shouldn't complete your plan as an adult, don't ask your children to, either. That's just begging for trouble.

Sanity Saving Checklist
☑ Are there enough hours in a day?
☑ Will it cause burnout?
☑ Are kids responsible?
☑ Are you expecting too much?
☑ Did you over-estimate mornings?
☑ Can they concentrate that long?
☑ Could you concentrate that long?
☑ Could you do it as an adult?

Appendix 1

Dealing with Homeschool Fatigue

Fatigue is the epic battle for homeschool parents. Often it's the biggest issue that homeschoolers face in the middle of winter. Between homeschooling and housework, parents feel stretched. Add your own need for self-care, the needs of your children and spouse, and it can feel impossible. Then add the darkness of winter months, and even seasoned veterans can be hanging on by a thread.

Yes, it's easy to become overwhelmed and fatigued! There are solutions that will help you face the day bravely, with the confidence and energy you need to make it through the year ... or at least until dinnertime. Hey, some ideas might even get you into the evening hours without a meltdown.

Put Priorities First

Every homeschool parent has a subject they don't understand, like, tolerate, or even remember to teach. When you identify your weak area, you can do something about it! Once you have identified your weak subject, remember to put that subject FIRST – it's the first thing your student does in the morning and then it's out of the way! You're not spending all day worrying about it or nagging your child to get that dreaded subject done!

Make sure it's always done and never missed. Prioritize it by also spending extra time and money on the weak area. A monetary investment in these weak areas has two potential benefits. First, it is human nature to value things more if we invest in them. Just the act of spending money can give you a lift in attitude. Believe it or not, the second benefit is that you may purchase a resource that makes the dreaded topic tolerable and dare I say ... fun! This strategy can eliminate a lot of stress and help prevent homeschool fatigue.

Enjoy Your Coffee

A cup of coffee or tea can be your inspiration for homeschool happiness. It can motivate you to have your morning meeting with your kids. When you meet with your children over a cup of coffee each day, and go over your expectations for them, the whole day will go more smoothly. A quick daily check-in is often all it takes. It reminds me a lot of having a quiet time. Your morning coffee can help you have your morning meeting with God. When you meet with the Lord each day, and He reveals His expectations for you, then your whole day will go more smoothly. A quick daily check-in with the Bible can be just the encouragement you need to stay on course.

Coffee can encourage you to take care of yourself. If you make time for self-care, you'll be much more capable of doing some other-care. We do so much for others all day long. A bit of "me time" can start the day off right. It doesn't have to be coffee, it can be tea or a warm meal, but taking care of you is the first step toward taking care of others. Remember what the airlines say, "First, put on your own oxygen mask."

Coffee can encourage budding friendships, if you can plan a coffee date with another homeschool mom. Instead of dropping children off at a play date, stay and enjoy fellowship with others. We often crave the company of someone other than our children, and sharing a coffee can encourage sharing our feelings. The best support system I had was my weekly cup of coffee with my best friend. She shared her struggles about learning disabilities, and I shared my woes about my own children. We both ended up with a better appreciation for the struggles others face.

Coffee can ensure you have margin. Everyone needs time in their day with nothing planned. The margin of your day is like the margins in a book. Book margins make a book readable, just as life margins make life livable. If you don't have time to sit down and have a cup of coffee, then you don't have enough margin in your life. Take a moment. Sip. Breathe. It's therapy. Your quiet moments of relaxation can give wonderful memories. I remember going to Starbucks once a week, while my son Kevin taught chess. It was just Alex and me in the coffee shop; he was studying and I was sipping my peppermint mocha learning about homeschooling high school. Good memories. Memories can last a lifetime.

Invest in Self Care

A healthy body is less fatigued, and more resistant to disease. To fight fatigue, eat healthy food and get regular rest at night. When you are tired, especially during seasons when you can't sleep all night, be sure to take a nap. Care for yourself, because your job is so important, and your children are counting on you to be healthy, rested, and responsive. That can't happen if you are exhausted, fatigued, or overly frustrated.

Care for yourself by scheduling some free time each day. Spend time with other moms. Share feelings with trustworthy friends. Having enough time to yourself will mean that you can't do it all alone. Delegate some responsibilities with your spouse and children. Delegation is not a sign of weakness; it's the sign of a leader. You are the leader of your home, and it's your job to delegate some tasks.

A healthy spiritual life can fight fatigue as well, giving you a sense of purpose and value. Have a regular quiet time each day, reading the Bible. Spend time praying and verbalizing your reliance on God as your source of strength.

Move More

Get your blood pumping. Do something to increase your blood flow. Little things can get your heart rate up. Regularly change your study location, moving from kitchen, to couch, to desk. Take regular breaks. Between books, or between courses, take a few minutes off.

Take five minutes to put in a load of laundry, or empty the dishwasher. Sure, it's just housework, but it's still a break from studying and teaching, and sometimes that's all you need. Drink a glass of water each hour. That will certainly get you up and moving more (at least to the bathroom!) and can increase your circulation.

Exercise can battle fatigue. Set aside time to exercise regularly. Perhaps you can exercise in the morning, before school starts. Maybe you can exercise in the afternoon, when older teens or your spouse can supervise quiet seatwork.

Take a quick walk. If you can't exercise, then just take a stroll around the yard or neighborhood. Don't call it exercise, just go outside and breathe the fresh air. A brisk walk, no matter how long or how short, can be rejuvenating, or at least wake you up enough to get your work done. Going outside is often the real cure for fatigue.

Vary the Routine

Once a day, try to mix in some fun activities. You might do a creative project or a hands-on activity. A fun activity might be a science experiment, an art project, or playing a musical instrument. Anything that is different from reading a book can provide stimulation. Try to do one creative or hands-on activity each day. During seatwork time, you can vary the routine by adding music.

Once a week, make it your goal to play. Schedule something fun to do and get out of the house. For some families, that might mean a long trip to town for groceries, or taking a quick stop at the park for fun. Another family might schedule a sports activity or meeting with friends each week. If you plan just one day away from home, it won't mess up your schedule, or keep you from completing your duties. On the other hand, if you are someone who is always running around, you don't need to do more playing than you already plan. This playtime doesn't have to take all day - it can take just an hour or so to make all the difference.

Once a month, consider taking a mental health day. All parents feel they can't take it sometimes. It's not a sign of weakness to need a day off. Schools regularly plan for mid-winter breaks because they know it's hard to stay focused during the dark months of winter. Take a break and give yourself a day off when you need it. People who work hard know the value of a true day of rest.

Appendix 2

Readers Sound-off on their Favorite Coping Strategies

Find a Coping Mechanism

Sitting back to relax with a warm cup of coffee or tea can help you take care of yourself. But my way of coping may not fit everyone. Create your own coping mechanism. We discussed our coping mechanisms on my Facebook page. "How do you cope with homeschool fatigue?" We got so many great suggestions, you are sure to find something that will help you today! I have collected the best ideas for this appendix. Enjoy!

"Change location, sunshine works best. Food throughout the day, coffee, yogurt fruit smoothies from blender, fresh carrot apple juice from juicer, breakfast, mid-morning snack, lunch, happy hour favorite fruit juice with cheese dip and tortilla chips, dinner, dessert. Run in the morning, walk the dog mid-day and before bed to find time alone with hubby, bike ride, whenever possible ... seeking healthy options."
~ Laura

"Exercise! I go for a walk alone every day once the school day is done. It's a great way for me to downshift from homeschool mom/teacher/principal/guidance counselor mode into a more relaxed 'just mom' mode."
~ Sonja

"Spending time with other homeschool moms. It refreshes my soul."
~ Laura

"To prevent burnout, I build some cushion into our schedule, allowing for one or two impromptu days off each month. I limit our outside activities while also trying to have at least one Sanity Day (full day at home) each week. Then if life gets too hectic or we are still facing burnout, I drop everything except the absolute essentials for a few days: reading great books, notebooking, basic math, and lots of nature study."
~ Rebecca

"Drop the 'studies' for a day, two or three - or a week, play, relax, go to the park and regroup. My kids love to color, so sometimes we just print a pile of coloring pages or paper dolls, let them create or play games, put on music or audio books and yes, naps are great if you can squeeze them in.

I guess my biggest strategy is really to do all of those things before any burnout sets in - like

sometimes a rainy day is just a cozy day to relax."
~ Galadriel

"Change of location. When we're getting burned out, we pack things up and study somewhere else. For us, that's usually the park. We sit in the car to read or do seat work. Then, they can play for a while (P.E.) before we head back. Sometimes we do nature walks for science, even if it doesn't go with that year's subject. Or, we do a field trip somewhere close. Though, I am working on getting better at field trips."
~ Carrie

"Taking probiotics at bedtime. And making sure I spend time with the Lord each day reading His word, definitely gives me a new perspective on things."
~ Heidi

"We take breaks every 6 weeks. We put the curriculum away and focus on our other interests like

art, movies, video games, shopping with friends, etc. There is still plenty of learning going on during this relaxed time."
~ Michelle

"Attending daily mass is a reminder for why I have children and why it is my responsibility to educate them. Thanks to God for the blessings he has given our family. I have two awesome teenage boys!"
~ Happy

"Going outside really helps me when I'm stressed or tired but still need to get school done. We have a hammock chair that I love or sometimes I just spread a sheet & bring a pillow."
~ Suzanne

"A quick workout during lunch break. And a big glass of water."
~ Sherry

"Bible lessons and drinking Virgil's Root Beer or Black Cherry Cream Soda."
~ Piety

"Chocolate with coffee. Taking a day off on occasion helps us all feel better. I can do chores, and my daughter can do whatever she feels like."
~ Stephanie

"While standing still and waiting on son to do a task, I have started to exercise: squats, leg kicks, do the grapevine, back kicks, walking in place, etc. Not only am I getting exercise, it is making me feel better and have more energy. GET MOVING!!"
~ Susan

"Park days with friends."
~ Jennifer

"Very important to spend time in prayer and Bible study. Also very important to have a time by yourself at least once a week."

~ Sandi

"Prayer and a white board with simple tasks that can be crossed off - helps me stay on target when too tired to hold it in my head!"
~ Debbie

"After lessons are done (and if I can swing it) I take a 30 minute nap. Also like to go outside with the brood for a walk."
~ Heather

"I've been homeschooling for 15+ years now with multiple children. Here are some things I've learned to combat fatigue: 1) Delegate, delegate, delegate. Mom does not have to do everything. 2) Perfectionism leads to fatigue. You, your house, your kids and your husband do not need to be perfect. 3) Plan time to take care of yourself. It's imperative to take care of your health. If you aren't healthy, it makes it difficult to take care of others. 4) Laugh ... often. The kids have created a disaster in

the family room, you burned dinner, and the baby just puked down your back. You can laugh, cry or get angry. Choose to laugh. It's really easy to get angry or cry. It takes an effort to look for the positives. Make the effort. You'll be happier about it and feel less burned out in general."
~ Erika

"Changing location. Move to the living room, kitchen, park, backyard, etc."
~ Cindy

"We have SOS days. (Save Our Sanity). A random day off of studies to go out and enjoy nature, or to watch old movies all day, or make stuff, or cook fun things we wouldn't normally make, etc. It's more for my sanity than theirs, but they do appreciate it."
~ Heidi

"1. Switch it up and plan a fun lesson. 2. Take a picnic lunch break, followed by a nature walk.

3. Use educational DVDs or audio books every so often. 4. Have an older child help a younger one. 5. Read poetry. It's soothing. 6. Keep on praying! 7. Don't let fear or guilt weigh you down. 8. Eat a healthy breakfast. 9. Finish your work in four days, and make Friday an enrichment day. 10. You will be tired from time to time. Just do what you can."
~ Heather

"Do one thing creative each day ... arrange some flowers ... drop someone a SHORT note ... pull together one page to scrapbook later ... pull together things for a handmade greeting card ... bake something to give to a neighbor. I'm in my 17th or 18th year of homeschooling and still struggle with tiredness at times."
~ Connie

"Definitely taking a day off to go do something fun. We have picture day in the fall, ice-skating in the winter and sometimes we'll curl up

with mugs of hot goodies and watch a movie. Moms need to have something that they enjoy doing and it doesn't have to be away from home. Having a definite stop and start time for school helps too and then you won't feel like that's all you do."
~ Tricia

"Nap! Have realistic expectations. Spend time with like-minded friends who can encourage you."
~ Mary Jo

"Don't be afraid to ditch curriculum that is just not working (or just take a break from it and rethink approach). Do things that you love to do as a family to recharge everyone's batteries."
~ Gail

"Praise music always helps me to power through it! Usually a day off to rest or catch up also alleviates some of the fatigue."
~ Autismland

"Delegating and asking for help are big ones (and hard to remember for me). Taking time off is also important. My hubby used to often walk in from work, look at my face, and send me to Books a Million for a cream soda and a book."
~ Tina

"When I need a break I exclaim, "Time for P.E.!" and send the kids to the backyard until further notice."
~ Ivette

"'Most important things.' For housework and for homeschool, I always have in mind what are the most important things, both for the long term and for the day, for each child. That way, if I don't get anything else done, I know I've done the things that matter most."
~ Rebecca

"Mani/pedi - so worth the $. Makes you feel like a girl (not just a mom)."
~ Theresa

"A day of scriptures, and fasting prayer, to ponder each child and then record inspirations/personal revelations I receive ... I notice for our family, burn out only happens when we lose sight/get off track, of what we were inspired to do in the first place ... amazing how easy it is to lose track of what is working, and slip into 'other things'."
~ Brenda

Afterword

Who is Lee Binz and What Can She Do for Me?

Number one best-selling homeschool author, Lee Binz is The HomeScholar. Her mission is "helping parents homeschool high school." Lee and her husband Matt homeschooled their two boys, Kevin and Alex, from elementary through high school.

Upon graduation, both boys received four-year, full tuition scholarships from their first choice university. This enables Lee to pursue her dream job - helping parents homeschool their children through high school.

On The HomeScholar website, you will find great products for creating homeschool transcripts and comprehensive records to help you amaze and impress colleges.

Find out why Andrew Pudewa, Director of the Institute for Excellence in Writing says, "Lee Binz knows how to navigate this often confusing and frustrating labyrinth better than anyone."

You can find Lee online at:

www.TheHomeScholar.com

If this book has been helpful, could you please take a minute to write us a quick review on Amazon?

Thank you!

Testimonials

"You Help Me Keep Focused!"

"I wanted to let you know how much I appreciate the Gold Care Club and how you have helped me keep focused. Last Friday, at our co-op, I shared with some high school homeschooling moms how happy I am with your service and help, and they are considering joining. I tell everyone I know about how you are helping me, because you truly are a gift from God. Because this homeschool high school college prep is scary! I also tell about your website and your products. May the Lord continue to bless you."

Blessings,
Susanne P.

"Immediately I Felt at Ease"

"Thank you for your help! I've told many of my homeschooling friends about you. You are kind and have such a heart to help. I wasn't sure what to expect when I made my first phone call with my questions. Immediately I felt at ease, like I was talking to a friend, a mentor.

I've so appreciated your encouragement these last couple of months. What was an overwhelming task got broken down into manageable pieces. Bit by bit the unbearable burden was lightened and lifted.

The wealth of information in your webinars and the baby steps you help us take make it so much easier. I love how you continue to educate yourself so you can teach us and guide those of us in the trenches. You are a lifeline!

I love all your Coffee Break Books. Again, bite size pieces which are manageable. But each bite is a nugget of wisdom!

Thank you for ALL you do."

~ Linda J. in New Jersey

For more information about my **Gold Care Club**, go to:

www.TheHomeScholar.com/Gold-Care.php

Also From The HomeScholar...

- The HomeScholar Guide to College Admission and Scholarships: Homeschool Secrets to Getting Ready, Getting In and Getting Paid (Book and Kindle Book)
- Setting the Records Straight - How to Craft Homeschool Transcripts and Course Descriptions for College Admission and Scholarships (Book and Kindle Book)
- Total Transcript Solution (Online Training, Tools and Templates)
- Comprehensive Record Solution (Online Training, Tools and Templates)

- Gold Care Club (Comprehensive Online Support and Training)
- Preparing to Homeschool High School (DVD)
- Finding a College (DVD)
- The Easy Truth About Homeschool Transcripts (Kindle Book)
- Parent Training A la Carte (Online Training)
- Homeschool "Convention at Home" Kit (Book, DVDs and Audios)

The HomeScholar "Coffee Break Books" Released or Coming Soon on Kindle and Paperback:

- Delight Directed Learning: Guiding Your Homeschooler Toward Passionate Learning
- Creating Transcripts for Your Unique Child: Help Your Homeschool Graduate Stand Out from the Crowd
- Beyond Academics: Preparation for College and for Life
- Planning High School Courses: Charting the Course Toward High School Graduation
- Graduate Your Homeschooler in Style: Make Your Homeschool Graduation Memorable

- Keys to High School Success: Get Your Homeschool High School Started Right!
- Getting the Most Out of Your Homeschool This Summer: Learning just for the Fun of it!
- Finding a College: A Homeschooler's Guide to Finding a Perfect Fit
- College Scholarships for High School Credit: Learn and Earn With This Two-for-One Strategy!
- College Admission Policies Demystified: Understanding Homeschool Requirements for Getting In
- A Higher Calling: Homeschooling High School for Harried Husbands (by Matt Binz, Mr. HomeScholar)
- Gifted Education Strategies for Every Child: Homeschool Secrets for Success
- College Application Essays: A Primer for Parents
- Creating Homeschool Balance: Find Harmony Between Type A and Type Zzz ...
- Homeschooling the Holidays: Sanity Saving Strategies and Gift Giving Ideas
- Your Goals this Year: A Year by Year Guide to Homeschooling High School

- Making the Grades: A Grouch-Free Guide to Homeschool Grading
- High School Testing: Knowledge That Saves Money
- Getting the BIG Scholarships: Learn Expert Secrets for Winning College Cash!
- Easy English for Simple Homeschooling: How to Teach, Assess and Document High School English
- Scheduling - The Secret to Homeschool Sanity: Plan You Way Back to Mental Health
- Junior Year is the Key to High School Success: How to Unlock the Gate to Graduation and Beyond
- Upper Echelon Education: How to Gain Admission to Elite Universities
- How to Homeschool College: Save Time, Reduce Stress and Eliminate Debt
- Homeschool Curriculum That's Effective and Fun: Avoid the Crummy Curriculum Hall of Shame!
- Comprehensive Homeschool Records: Put Your Best Foot Forward to Win College Admission and Scholarships
- Options After High School: Steps to Success for College or Career

- How to Homeschool 9th and 10th Grade: Simple Steps for Starting Strong!
- Senior Year Step-by-Step: Simple Instructions for Busy Homeschool Parents
- High School Math The Easy Way: Simple Strategies for Homeschool Parents In Over Their Heads

Would you like to be notified when we offer the next *Coffee Break Books* for FREE during our Kindle promotion days? If so, leave your name and email below and we will send you a reminder.

http://www.TheHomeScholar.com/ freekindlebook.php

Visit my Amazon Author Page!

amazon.com/author/leebinz

CPSIA information can be obtained at www.ICGtesting.com
Printed in the USA
LVOW10s1445070316

478097LV00056B/1243/P